Imaginary Maps

Imaginary Maps

Darrell Epp

Carolyn Marie Souaid, Editor

Signature
EDITIONS

Cover design by Doowah Design.

This book was printed on Ancient Forest Friendly paper.
Printed and bound in Canada by Marquis Book Printing Inc.

Acknowledgements
Some of these poems first appeared in the following magazines:
Poetry Ireland, Poetry Nottingham, Maisonneuve, subTerrain, Chiron Review, Tears In The Fence, Santa Clara Review, Whitewall Review, Wisconsin Review, Saranac Review, Homestead Review, Roanoke Review, Mannequin Envy, Splizz, H, The Street, POEM, Aries, Freefall (US), *Freefall* (Canada), *Fire, Latino Stuff Review, Nexus, Freexpression, Permafrost,* and *Grain.*

We acknowledge the support of The Canada Council for the Arts and the Manitoba Arts Council for our publishing program.

Library and Archives Canada Cataloguing in Publication

Epp, Darrell, 1972-
    Imaginary maps / Darrell Epp.

Poems.
ISBN 978-1-897109-32-8

    I. Title.

PS8559.P72I43 2009   C811'.6   C2009-901811-X

Signature Editions
P.O. Box 206, RPO Corydon, Winnipeg, Manitoba, R3M 3S7
www.signature-editions.com

Contents

Mission Statement

the disease of consciousness
and all that it requires:
nurses telling me to relax,
musty four-colour newsprint,
prophecies unheeded
and promises unkept,
books packed with lies,
memories of redwoods,
mistakes on auto-repeat, your
woefully underwritten third act,
my unquenchable hatred
for whoever ruins a mystery
by solving it,
that first kiss and
the downhill slide,
the mathematical
laws that bind us,
twin sisters named
hope and rage, vagrants
i mistake for vampires,
trichinosis,
all of it and
always the
terrible whiteness of
the empty screen, a
burden too heavy
to put down.

What I'm Quoting From

it's the mistakes
and the things that never even happened
that really jump out at you,
my every movement
is a quotation from a children's book,
you know the one, with the astronaut
and the dragon on the cover?
no one ever died from love
in the movies but i'm not sure i'm even here,
regarding action or reaction
i'm a have-not,
unable to attack or defend
against fate's hurricanes,
sometimes i think
the big bang never ended,
sometimes there's just
the bride of frankenstein
in the wal-mart, sighing
at the high cost of living,
vacantly admonishing her
gasping asthmatic progeny.

For H.P. Lovecraft

From even the greatest horrors irony is seldom absent.

were you right? must everything we say
mean something else? even in our most
urgent moments, must every face be a
mask, every smile a fanged attack?
she came and she went and i said the
world will keep turning and everything
will be fine, but that's not what i meant
to say, that wasn't what i thought at all.
howard — all the way down to china
i can feel the grooves of your fingerprint,
i can hear your echoing mocking laughter.

Valentine

one mirror
batteries not included.
a staircase of smoke

ascending into nowhere.
the dreams of a cloud.
a surgeon removes a

tumour while blindfolded.
you want a baby but have
to settle for a spider plant.

the stars look so cute from
the balcony, up close they're
spinning screaming hells.

when we run out of words
we realize we don't need
words. let's stay in tonight,
this town is full of pickpockets.

Elephant

off-screen a storm is brewing:
the challenge; the long walk;
the showdown; the sundown;
the end. i wish i had an enemy
so i could challenge him to a duel.

hit pause, pray for strength. six-
guns twirling in the sun always
remind me of halloween 1983,
always crush me with a nostalgia
stronger than gravity on jupiter.

all these cowboys died before
i was born. i've never touched
a horse. i have a nickname:
my friends call me "elephant."
that's because i never forget.

The Night That Doesn't End

we grow bored trying to figure out
whose fault it is. going for a walk
downtown is more logical. fuzzy stars,
ghost of a moon. tomorrow's headlines
are tattooed on the neck of a passerby.
the news is all bad. you tell me we have
problems communicating and i agree,
that's the one thing we can agree on.
christmas lights crown the lamp-
posts a week into spring, someone
should write a letter to city hall.
motivational self-help messages
blare out of a taxi. buds burst
in the towers made of flowers. an
actor slowly raises his mask, strobes
like a pulsar and disappears. that
noise, is that angel language or just
an insect screaming in my ear?
downtown is really the place to be.
hard to believe all this could ever be
forgotten. now it's time to cry over
chicken biryani spicy enough to
make strangers ask "where's the funeral?"
they can't ever say we didn't try our best.

Fragment

my dark-eyed queen
wanted a man,
not an apology.

For Jane

i step out of the ford f-150
to admire the lunar eclipse.
it's a scary shade of red. i'll
see another one when i'm
old but i'll never see jane
again. there's a hole in my
pocket. i lost two dimes today.
when i go home after work no
one will be there to ask me for
anything. the moon is pulling
away from us, three inches a year,
because of tides and gravity. that's
a fact, jane told me all about it.

Frozen Moments

it would get cold and stay
cold, we'd never get a break

grass slept under a white blanket;
mothers told their kids to shut up

bears slept for 5 months at a time and
i went 5 days 3 hours without sleeping

having broken my record, i
felt proud but also confused

i was trying to decide, eggs scrambled
or fried, bacon or ham, when

you took off your jacket and stuffed
a snowball down my shirt

such a funny thing for you to do
when we were already so cold.

Pinned, Curious

a charlie brown cartoon pinned
to the fridge by a force called
magnetism

me, pinned to the couch
by a force called
gravity

kyla's out of codeine
somehow it's my fault

i've heard that mouse in
my wall for so long it's
time i gave him a name

what's it like to live
inside the wall?

is it too late for
me to start over,

too soon to make jokes
about the end of the world?

The Pie In The Sky

our dirty forks in the sink,
their overlapping handles
forming a flattened x

a room away, after
playing naked twister
we dream of a road
leading to a city built on

a cloud where nobody
ever has to kiss a lover
goodbye since everything
has already been paid for.

Now Slips Away

the wolf-man scans the night sky
but the air's metallic haze makes
every full moon a surprise, folks
hate the factory smokestacks but
need the jobs, have you ever
noticed how every little thing has
an evil twin? the crime scene is
being cordoned off, the wedding
ring pawned. we exiled the
constellations in exchange for
profit-sharing and a fat pension.
a set of habits is mistaken for a life.
we work eat sleep and not much else.
a co-worker's wife turned out to be
a robot, having started to rust around
the tear ducts: what had tasted like
true love, mere algorithm.
night's engine hums, clicks as
it changes gears. like a nothing
instead of everything, Now slips
away without anyone noticing.
trapped between here and where
you fight the urge to walk when
the little man says don't walk,
to scream at the oncoming trucks
sophie, babe, i take it all back.
randomness is the illusion, this
must be some sort of test, it
must all add up to something.
the registered nurse shivering
at the bus stop on the edge of
something new, saying nothing
to no one; the cathedral full of
relics secret and vital: the no
trespassing sign on the door.

How Many Molecules

…the insomniac is
counting molecules,
digesting a burrito
with difficulty.
what's your infinity
multiplied by my zero?
existential is a word you
might use for tonight. the
sizzling bacon, the hum of
nocturnal motors, the
mind too big for its brain.
tragedies hibernate inside
moments like these: the
bloody wedding dress,
the mushroom clouds,
pianos thrown off the
balcony. what to
say, and to whom.

Bird Watching

a platoon of retirees feeds the birds
just past the DO NOT FEED THE
BIRDS sign. the ground is spongy.
ribbons of fog rise from the marsh.
someone snaps a photograph. the
birds are hungry. or maybe just lazy.
things can go from cute to nasty
faster than a blink; a goose and
a duck start squabbling over the same
piece of rye bread, the viciousness
delivers a little shock. we turn
back toward the car, it's hard not to
think of all our unspeakable shared
moments, the ticking stopwatch.
light as a ghost, you touch my arm
and say son, i just don't want you
to make the same mistakes i did.

Tribute

lightning flashes
in the greenest eyes

her old-woman hands
slicing a chicken

the sound of a door
opening then closing

forever (nobody else
there to hear it)

all gone now, only the
Idea of her remains

you can buy all these
memories plus etc.

in return for the power
to fix things, i need help

filling these blank pages.

What Johanna Said

the sky is tattooed with the signature of
God.
like acrobats,
clouds tumble from one end of the world's
roof to the other, just as they would if the
earth were flat.
rare jewels shatter in the rip tide,
bursts of amethyst and onyx as
big as my eyes.
i lack the vocabulary
for so many of
the very best things.
pedestrians have gone extinct.
kids have play-dates
instead of play. the
actors won't know if they're in a comedy
or a tragedy until it's time to take a bow.
meaning peeks out of every window in a
thousand different shades of white. infinite
joy, your eyelash on my shoulder.
there are times when all you get
is the answering machine as
the screaming match
between different gravities
continues; whether it's noise
or music depends on
the listener.
a neighbour baking
samosas smiles
at a childhood memory.
the smell reminds me
of what johanna used to say
that special word she used—
what was it?

For Susan

an insect-eyed vagrant
crept thru the parking lot, care-
fully pinning a maple leaf under
the windshield wiper blade of
every parked car until a guy
returning to his suv said: hey!

the leaf man said to the car man,
maple leaves come from maple trees,
maple syrup comes from maple trees,
i remember susan, susan was such a
sweetheart, susan had pancakes for
breakfast and put so much maple syrup
on them i thought she was going to be sick,

but that happened a very long time ago,

i wouldn't expect you to remember.

Stab

forgotten:
a dusty attic containing a cute
outfit purchased to impress
on the first day of school
and
a toy f-16 fighter jet, never
played with, still in the box,
someone had grown "too old
for toys" two weeks before
getting it as a birthday gift.

last friday
i got lost in a strange part of
town, all the houses looked the
same, all the people seemed so
happy, i said

"if i could go back and change things"

and i didn't start to cry, i started to
hurry, started to sweat, i imagined
the beads of sweat poking me
in the back were knives, the tiny
knives of little assassins.

Already Lost

asking to have the paper read
to her when there's nothing
stopping her from picking it
up and reading it herself

it's like you hear but you don't listen

wondering about all the animals
that live in the walls and under
the floor, remembering flying a
a kite like it was all that mattered

or you listen but you don't hear or

learning not to smile or look at
their faces or most importantly
their eyes, look them in
the eye and you've already lost.

Retro Café

off-screen, a match is lit.

your shaky hand spills coffee.

"i don't think you can truly understand
dostoyevsky until you've had your heart
broken and set on fire, then everything
becomes as simple as checkers—"

look i really hate to interrupt, you
being suicidal and all,

but what is it with this place?

isn't our waitress the girl
king kong fell in love with?

isn't that busboy one of the little rascals?

isn't the bartender the pie-in-the-face man
in all those classic comedies?

doesn't the owner look like the fat man
from the maltese falcon?

and aren't you dietrichson, the luckless
husband from double indemnity,
directed by billy wilder,
1944?

Perennial

alien toenails in the sink, drops of blood
in the soap dish, a fly in the ointment.
clean-up time again, but what year is it?
my ribs snapped like dry twigs beneath

your straitjacket hugs. our first-date
theatre is now a parking lot. tomorrow
i'll try shaving with a shovel. green lights
make me stop. eating makes me hungry.

each departure becomes a return to this, a
private blizzard in red and white. i have a
super-power, my eyes can see through this
wall, right to where you are. that skirt really

doesn't match those shoes. special thanks
to the "b" that turned "one" into bone. your
photo fell so gently into the garbage can.
it's clean-up time again, but what year is it?

This Absence

trees with leaves like tin foil,
the ache of yesterday's
pleasures remembered,
plus all the rest of it tied
up in a boy scout knot.

clear skies and days that
end with a "y" so far away,
life is harder than it looks.
this absence will outlive
me, nothing ever ends.

Patience

four walls and a roof that leaks,
cobwebs in my skull, a bible on
the chair and nothing on the wall
where your picture used to hang.
yet man is born unto trouble as
the sparks fly upward, that's what
job said during his time of testing.
job had to endure a lot but at least
he never had to meet you, my dear.

Watching the Snow Melt While Trying to Make a Decision

a droplet of rusty water
in bayfront park
slides off an icicle,
bellyflops into lake
ontario. a finger
of heat writes its
name in the snow.
just one cloud today,
its octopus tentacles
unfurl until it resembles
a question mark. i have
more than one question.

For My Pharmacist

it's the longest night of the year
and i need to hear her approaching
footsteps like a toothache needs a tooth.

the fact that in an empty hotel room
there's no record of the catastrophic
winter nights we spent there bothers me
more than world wars 1 and 2 put together.

a strange man holding a cup of coffee
smiles at her with dazzling too-white teeth.

if only (big if) i could remember how to
spell xanax backwards, the gates might hold.

What Happened?

boil off the fat and here's what's
left: a midnight raccoon ripping into
my garbage bag, his eyes flashing
like supernovae in the baleful
glare of passing headlights. the

21st century: a windswept mess nobody
wants to clean up, the same insomnia,
the same filthy claws, the same missing
pieces. i was hoping for more: where
are the flying cars we were promised

in the 50s? where are the wisdom-dispensing
alien monoliths? where is my robot butler?
where is the one who, after my hard day
on the martian colony, removes my jet
pack and says hi, sweetie, how was your day?

Kissing Piranhas

"it's not what you meant to do,
 it's what you did that i don't like"
is what you say in front of the bingo
parlour and hey, how many bingo

parlours does one downtown need?
the cars all wish they were horses.
the trains wish they were mighty
godzillas. and what do you wish?

to be a cockroach, with your bones
on the outside, your thin skin under
a hard shell? that might work better
for you than zoloft and/or placebos,

but i'm no doctor. piranhas french-
kiss in water that's risen to my
knees and i'm not going anywhere:
everybody knows i was here first.

For Henry Ford

you look up at the ceiling and
your laughter like the braying
of a mule reminds me of a
german girl i knew 6 years
ago—in fact, you seem
identical to her in every way

i once worked in a canning
factory, we mass-produced
sliced pears packed in syrup,
i can't say how many identical
tins i saw rush by on tiny tracks
that summer, i never knew
whether i found that parade
of efficiency reassuring or
frightening

i think the assembly line
virus gave us something and
took something else away

when you go, please don't
slam the door, and if you
see the next one, tell her to
be kind to me, like you were.

For My Dad

going too fast in the slow lane
on the queen's highway the
brake lights ahead remind me
of a book about the grand
canyon i read when i was six. i miss
being a kid. i miss my dad. two
lanes merge into one as uniforms
snap pictures of an upside-down
ford explorer, shattered glass
crackles under my tires.
my dad never read poetry.

The Greyhound

our sixth winter nears and
all i ever get is the
occasional "sounds good"
or "not bad." I'd hoped
for more, something tree-
shaped, pointing up into
the future — but
i can't see in or out. you
put black tape over the
windows and before our
visitors arrive you turn
me into a hound baying
in the backyard, the rope
choking me tethered
securely to what i can't tell.

Mea Culpa!

andrea and i used to score together
she was so beautiful and now she's
completely gakked-out her hair and
teeth have started to fall out she's in
a hospital and won't be out soon i'm
shaking we thought what we were
doing really meant something what if
those clean and punctual folks we were
rebelling against actually had a point
it's enough to make me want to burn
my records and run back to the church
basement shave my head and join a
monastery stagger naked through the
sands like the old desert saints i'd like
to find some middle ground between
two extremes but i remember my dad
telling me that the middle of the road
is a great place to get run over and he
thought i never heard a word he said.

For Melanie

now

"i don't want to take the pill anymore," she
says. tomorrow's garbage day, if we don't
clean up now the trash will just sit here all
week long, there's a banana peel on the floor.

i wish one of us i don't care who would
take out the garbage. i wish i were reading
raymond chandler. i wish he'd written more
books. who do i wish i was? robert mitchum.

then

melanie and i went up to the roof and
danced like robots, it's harder than it
sounds. the constellations were better
than fireworks, we wished we could fly.

later there was no hard news anywhere,
the britney spears haircut was on every
channel as i wondered: why don't any
girls think the three stooges are funny?

Looking For a Break

i want to rid myself of
these clingy werewolves.

i'm losing it, i loathe their stink,
their atonal chanting, the way
they always answer a question
with another question.

i had a date last night, they
ruined it, i don't know why
that pleased them so much.

i'm a hairy guy i guess
but i'm not one of them

no matter what they say.

i swear i'm going to shave
every werewolf, stab
every vampire, fashion
the sun into a halo for myself.

i want to fly past the tides
and calendars and see a
new world with new eyes,
i want to start again.

For England

lovely queen victoria can't
beat my straight, nervously
unclasps her brassière

as rottweilers lick clean
our plates and old dead
albert shouts in protest.

"i say, there are limits…"

staring at lands
upon which the
sun never sets i
don't think of rhodes
or livingston, all i
can remember is
the 5th of november.

Sidewalk Trip

goth kids strut past like nazis. my father's eyes
glare at me from between two clouds, one looking
like a 2-headed dog, the other like ronald reagan.

that scratchy sound planets make as they push
against emptiness, it's a kind of music, i strain
to catch the melody, i want to sing along.

the sidewalk chills my ass, behind me st. john
the evangelist reaches his stone arms out to me,
i want to give him a hug, tell him i know what

it's like to be misunderstood but i remember
all the people and all the ghosts of the people
who came before them as my blood delivers

the rest of the dose to my brain and i just let go.

Zombie

legacies of her watermelon-
scented hair still cling to these
walls — wow look at
that! five months after she
was last here or anywhere
near here not much has
changed i cleaned the
place up it just got dirty
again. i still love staring
out this window at everything
from the pedestrians to the
clouds. across the avenue
the same lime-coloured
pulsing neon is trying to
hypnotize me 4 nights out
of 7 i don't resist i think
i'm entitled to a little some-
thing and oh here it comes
it's just like a warm bath.

Comparatively Speaking

a mind as empty as a jack o' lantern

a child as discarded as 1999's calendar

a punch line as funny as a broken condom

a moment as sad as paying for it on valentine's day

a concept as smart as bringing bottled water
to the underwater kingdom of atlantis

an idea as bright as that time you took a hair
dryer along on our trip to jupiter: just where exactly
did you think you were going to plug it in?

For the Days

when nothing's done for the first time.

traffic's so slow even the snails
are passing me. i'm late horny
hungry. the antenna's gone, my
radio's caught between two
stations, heavy metal on one,
tomorrow's genocide on the other.

i know this song i know it from before—

you think you got it rough, said
the spider to the fly, try being a
calendar salesman in january.

Imaginary Maps

i do adore the aquamarine
network of veins stamped
on your left torso; it looks
like a spider web, it looks
like someone tattooed you
a map. a pirate's buried
treasure map is what i'm
thinking of. ahoy mateys,
yon comely maiden will
lead us to a king's ransom
in spanish doubloons, that's
what all the pirates would
shout in unison, foul-
mouthed parrots perched
on every other shoulder.

Wrong Number

you told me never to call you again
so of course i called you again and
again just another "guy thing" i
wouldn't expect you to understand
i was stoned i got the numbers all
mixed up the woman only spoke
french and was as nice as could be
expected under the circumstances
i still remember the sound of her
voice some humbling fundamental
human goodness poked through the
language barrier and i hope that
woman has a nice day i hope she
lives to be a hundred and twenty.

For a Sick Friend

aggressively competing with
the urge to write something
is the urge to write nothing,
record nothing, to tie my
hands behind my back and
sew my lips shut, to quit
adding to this stack of poems
that will never help anyone as
much as you've helped me.

For the Exes

you ask me to describe what i'm feeling.
it would be easier for me to describe a
spiral staircase without using my hands.

instead:

i saw something today that nobody else
saw, a raccoon so beautiful and split in
two, it looked so strange almost glowing
i wanted to pick it up and hug it like a
baby, the important stuff you just can't
learn from the encyclopedia britannica.

i walked on, on to the post office as

scavenger birds screamed with delight

but don't worry too much, the sunny
spring-bringing sun shone on and on.

can you spot this poem's hidden message?

Rise Above

from way up here
i can hear the telephone
from the time you hung up on me
and a congregation from thirty
years ago chanting hymns in unison
like androids

i can see you dancing in the snow
(you look like an angel)
and our old addresses in
obsolete phone books,
letters unsent,
letters returned,
current address
unknown.

King St. E. Blues

belligerent panhandlers frighten old
women, the buildings move closer,
squeeze alleyways and streets by
a few millimetres at a time and if
anybody notices, nobody's talking.

downtown mondays are brutal, mysterious.
last monday they caught a guy stuffing a
fetus into a garbage can, they say he'll
probably get life, failure to recycle is a
serious thing nowadays. the air tastes like

rusted staples and flat pepsi. i miss you,
but i'm glad you're not here. i'm as guilty
as anybody but all i can do is wonder what
it's like on the other side of the clouds,
count to ten, start over, try again tomorrow.

You Know What I Mean

the prettiest girl you've
walked past in weeks
on the arm of some
shaved gorilla in a cowboy hat
who will never appreciate her
on as many levels as you can
blah blah blah

hollywood doing tacky remakes
of all your favourite old classics

phone numbers you can't remember,
faces you can't forget, and

other things that make
you laugh and/or cry.

Mystery Guest

the worst part is the way the ladies
laugh at every joke he makes.
everyone wants to touch him.
he doesn't wear a shirt, his jewelry
is blindingly reflective. he laughs,
says, hey i just give the people what
they want, i never force them to do
anything, man. his tongue is scaly, like
an iguana's, prehensile like a chimp's
tail. he doesn't blink. i'm not even sure
he has eyelids. i ask who invited him.
you: i thought he was a friend of yours...

For Frank R.

calluses on his hand
like spots on the sun,
a soul too big for any
temporary body or box.
i always pay the phone
bill a day late. what began
as a matter of principle
now commemorates our
last late-night conversation,
"read it again; just trust me"
is what he'd said so i do
through all the empty weeks,
i'm alive and impatient and
grateful for the night, for the
dreams in which he cameos.

Revenge

it's a terrible thing to admit

but 9 times out of 10

it wasn't about "making love"

it was about making a point, it was
about getting back at all those vague
preppy girls who had ignored me in
high school so many years ago

she'd ask me what i was thinking about

and i'd say nothing

or, alternately

the word "nothing"

then she'd laugh and call me
a funny little monkey
and she'd be right,
as always.

Remembering It

there's no point in
wondering or missing it, when
something's over it's over, and
the older i get the harder it is to
believe it happened at all;
i go to bed so early now, there
were good things about it but
my body just remembers the
bad, the dry heaves, the stomach
pains, the bulging insect eyes;
i still smile thinking about
the fearlessness, the stupidity,
how we'd stagger
around like roman centurions,
victorious invaders, and now
this town feels as lonely as the
moon—where did everybody
go, man?

last i heard, gerald was still the
same, he's probably the saddest
one of us all, except for tim,
a telemarketing tv addict
so angry it hurts to look at him,
but you, i don't know about— are
you dead or alive or just some-
body's husband? does the room
you're in right now feel a
bit too small for you?

i know what you mean.

For Burt Lancaster

i'd been trying to discard my
belief in God but couldn't
do it, everything was just too noisy
too crazy, too obscene, too perfect

burt lancaster was busting out
of prison in black and white,
someone said to change the
channel but nobody did, he
deserved a chance after all
the crap they'd thrown at him

lou spoke of lorraine and her
wild ways, my heart stopped
beating and started back up at
1:01, stopped and started again
at 2:43 and people still say
nothing interesting ever goes
on in this town, how wild is that?

Alchemy

such a miracle, the sensation
of your hand resting on mine

the sky darkens and spits
but nothing can stop us

afterwards, when every
cloud cat dog bus car
or newspaper headline
reminds me of it, it's
almost hard to believe

i'd felt like water becoming
steam, lead becoming
gold in the occult blast
furnace inside of your heart.

For John Wayne

black and white movie
in which a cowboy hat

stalks and eventually
blows away his bank-

robbing twin brother.
the hats are cool but it's

the supporting characters
i really notice: empty

shot glasses (hats drink
straight from the bottle),

pistols that giggle
to each other when the

sheriff isn't looking,
sweaty garter belts,

the mob of grandfather
clocks chattering with

both hands over their faces.

Kitchen Angel

balsamic something, arugula
and sprouts, cherry tomatoes,
chopped onions, other things
nutritious and so mysterious.

i've been eating out of frozen
boxes for centuries; i feel like
an unthawed caveman
meeting his guardian angel.

you start to list the secret
ingredients that make the
dressing sing but i beg you
please don't tell me.

i don't want to know how
the magician made the statue
of liberty disappear.
i don't want to know how
the story ends.
i don't want to know what
you're thinking, i want
be endlessly surprised by
your unsolvable mystery.

Our Beach

The writhing waves lunge toward us
like clouds on methamphetamine

farther out it's so still and rhythmic,
like a pulse inside a womb, and it's
strange, almost scary; you wonder
why the edge of something so
serene should look so angry

wind and waves knock
the seagulls around but
they're used to it, it's
what they were made for

it's so loud! you shout, and
i wish we'd brought food,
i hope we stay together,
i feel so close to you it's
like i am you, i realize
suddenly how happy i
am because every wave that
hits the sand feels like
a beginning.

For Raymond Chandler

nervously we conspire
on a mattress on the floor
bills must be paid but "jobs"
is beginning to sound like
a vicious joke and then

i see on the bookshelf behind
you sideways beautiful words
the little sister
the high window
the long goodbye
farewell my lovely

it works so well it's scary
the pulse slows the born-
again morning starts fiat
luxing into the room's
every crevasse and corner

in falsetto you start to sing
an old favourite i sing along
until we change the world

your echo overlapping mine olympus
on one side kilimanjaro on the other
we could be superman's children or
anything at all just say the word babe.

I Want To Do My Part

flotillas of clouds streak by
without a care in the world,
nature can be such a show-off.

millions of birds and billions
of insects hatch secret plots
in their own animal languages.

i want to make dorothee pregnant,
want to watch our baby suckle her
breast for infinity plus a day, amen.

My Play

o how i wish my work was my
play. square pegs could fit into

round holes, the chicken could
trade places with the egg.

boots on my head, hats on my
feet, the evil queen becomes

the slave girl birthing new
stars inside the eagle nebula.

if i could show you exactly
how gorgeous you are as

you stagger sleepily out of
the bedroom and ask what's

for breakfast, nothing would
ever get done around here.

Everything Is Political

talked about the election for ten
minutes, then jokingly asked if
i was boring her. yes, she came
right out and said, she was just being
nice, pretending to be interested. i
said, "how can you not be interested
in this?!" she said, "i guess i'm just
not political." i think everything is
political so i said, "what should i do
the next time you're talking about
something boring, do i tell you or do
i pretend to be interested?" as the guy
at the next booth slammed down his
ketchup bottle and said, "i swear, becky,
sometimes it's like you think you're the
only girl in this town, well i got news for
you, you ain't!" william s. burroughs once
asked, "what came first, the intestine or
the tapeworm?" and I thought I knew
what he meant as the bill arrived and
dorothee whispered, "don't leave too
much of a tip; she doesn't deserve it."

While You Were Gone

the same 26 letters can be
rearranged in so many
different ways it almost
makes you drunk to think
about it until you think
about the dna, 4 amino
acids combined over &
over again in so many
different ways without
any repeats, you never
run into any doubles,
everybody—pedestrian
or rider—is a new miracle.
this is just something i
was thinking about as
i waited impatiently for
you to return from your
too-long vacation,
dreams of you are like
little balls of opium, all
arranged neatly in a row,
it's the waking up that hurts.

My Sky

thank You for my balcony
from which i watch light
and heat cook up colours
far beyond any categories.

between the sun and here,
bloody clouds like violent
undiscovered continents
tie themselves into knots

in discursive slow motion.
crazy spears of light shoot
out of the cumulus in
ways both terrifying and

reassuring. time slows.
ants feast on a blob
of spilled salsa by my
foot. all poems are prayers.

Morning Miracle

by degrees
the red baby sun sizzles the haunches of a cloud
while everyone, in unison, ponders how nothing
ever ends and everything always changes
and how innocent, or is that guilty,
we all undeniably are
until with mathematical inevitability
noise becomes music as a grace note
wrestles a loose improv into a masterpiece,
suffusing every transaction and every leaky
faucet with an accidental choreography, a
numinous kindness, and for a moment at least
we recognize ourselves in each other's faces,
we know what we mean. all
this happened yesterday, too.

Happy Ending

3 or 4 years ago my entire
life fit inside a ziploc bag.

now
i've started cycling and writing again,
and my life is too big to be contained
inside any container i've ever seen.

and the universe, which weighs more
than i can guess, fits quite comfortably
inside my brain, which only weighs
3 lbs.—it's a miracle!

you're inside here, too.

Index

Eco-Audit

Printing this book using Rolland Enviro 100 Print
instead of virgin fibres paper saved the following resources:

Trees	Solid Waste	Water	Air Emissions	Natural Gas
2	51 kg	4,821 L	112 kg	7 m³